# Witney and Bella's Lost and Found

Written by Zoë Clarke

Illustrated by Felicia Whaley

## Collins

This is Witney.

**Witney**

**Age** nine

**Likes** Boscoe

**Job** lost and found agent

This is Boscoe.

**Boscoe**

**Age** eight

**Likes** Witney

**Job** catching, fetching, itching

3

Witney and Boscoe are at Reeva's pie shop.

In the window there are pictures of lost things.

LOST

trolley

cage

Little April

keys

Witney and Boscoe are searching for Little April.

Let's fetch the finding kit!

This is Witney's finding kit.

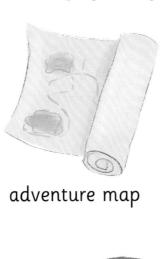

adventure map

little blanket

long cable

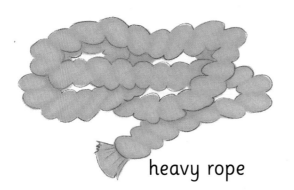

heavy rope

bag for clues

Witney snatched the washing bag by mistake!

Hurry, Boscoe!

Witney opened the bag.

There was an apron with large pockets.

They trudged across the wide bridge.

These might be the next clue! They are very large.

park

The large paw prints led to a giant ditch.

We need the long cable!

Witney looked in the bag.

There were eight stripy socks.

Witney made a giant sock rope and tied it to a huge tree.

She grabbed Boscoe and jumped!

Witney looked in the bag.

There were matching jumpers.

That's strange.

They put the matching jumpers on their heads.

Little April's coat! Fetch it, Boscoe.

Boscoe snatched the coat.
There was Little April! April was not little.

We need the heavy rope.

Witney looked in the bag.

There was a tie and some tights.

Witney pulled Little April.
Little April was very heavy.

Push, Boscoe!

The bag was empty, but Boscoe found
the park map and the trolley!

20

Witney put Boscoe and Little April in the trolley.

Just the keys and cage to find. Maybe tomorrow!

# Adventure map

#  After reading

**Letters and Sounds:** Phase 5

**Word count:** 294

**Focus phonemes:** /ai/ a, eigh /ee/ e-e, ey, e, y /oo/ u /igh/ ie, y /ch/ tch, t /j/ g, ge, dge /l/ le

**Common exception words:** of, to, the, are, one, were, their

**Curriculum links:** PSHE

**National Curriculum learning objectives:** Reading/word reading: apply phonic knowledge and skills as the route to decode words; read accurately by blending sounds in unfamiliar words containing GPCs that have been taught; read common exception words; read other words of more than one syllable that contain taught GPCs; read aloud accurately books that are consistent with their developing phonic knowledge; re-read books to build up their fluency and confidence in word reading; Reading: comprehension: link what they have read or hear read to their own experiences; discuss word meanings; discuss the significance of the title and events

## Developing fluency

- Take it in turns with your child to read a page each. Model reading with fluency and expression.
- Look through the book. Find and read the common exception words.
- Practise reading the speech bubbles aloud using expression. How would Witney would say these things?

## Phonic practice

- Look through the book together. Ask your child:
  - Can you spot words with the /j/ sound written in different ways? (*giant, large, strange, huge, cage, trudged, bridge, hedge*)
  - Can you spot words with the /ch/ sound? (*itching, snatched, ditch, fetching, scratchy, matching, catching*)

## Extending vocabulary

- Ask your child:
  - On page 10, the author uses the word **trudged**. Can you think of any other words you could use here? (e.g. *walked, marched, trekked, hiked, strolled*)
  - What does the word **strange** mean? (e.g. *unusual, not usual, different, peculiar, odd*)